eff-able

a spicy anthology of queer crip poetry

edited by JP Seabright & George Violet Parker

First published in 2025 by Fourteen Publishing.
fourteenpoems.com

Edited by JP Seabright and George Violet Parker
effable.uk

Design and typeset by Stromberg Design.
strombergdesign.co.uk

Proofreading and copy editing by Lara Kavanagh.
lk-copy.com

Printed by P2D Ltd, Westoning, Bedfordshire, UK.

ISBN: 978-1-0684951-2-0

CONTENTS

INTRODUCTION

Desire lines run throughout this little book of queer crip joy – the desires of queer disabled people; the editors' desires to read really good, really horny poetry; and our equivalent desire to lift up and celebrate the voices and experiences of our community. *eff-able* was birthed into being from this exchange between the editors in October 2023:

> *I reckon we should stop beating about the bush (fnar fnar) and just do a collab of rude sex poems. No idea who'd publish it, but it would be fun!*

> *My first response was 'thanks for not making me beg' so fnar fnar indeed! I'd love to!*

After a couple of weeks passing our own rudest and crudest sex poems back and forth like teenage boys passing dirty notes in class, we'd honed the idea:

> *Let's make it queer crip neurospicy sex, otherwise it's too broad. Author needs to identify as queer and crip/mad etc and it's an anthology of queer crip neurodiverse sexiness.*

> *Ughhhhhh yes!*

And thus, this anthology was born.

Self-confessed Poetry Pervs we are, but surely not the only ones? We wanted to read explicit erotica in excellent poetic form, but we also wanted representation on the page. To promote the voices of those who share our own experiences of sex and erotic embodiment within a queer, disabled, neurodivergent, and chronically ill body.

We searched for it, but were left wanting. This dearth of direct sexiness or erotica in poetry was the impetus for this collection. Erotica is often considered 'less than', not an appropriate topic for 'serious' poetry, or is shoved into that dismissive category of 'confessional poetry'.

We made lists, shared voice notes, and started getting hot under the collar about how this would be an amazing, vibrant, and damn sexy anthology – but also so much more. From the outset, spotlighting and supporting queer crip poets has been central to this project. We know ourselves how difficult it is to engage and be part of the 'scene' when it isn't always possible to leave the house. How poetry events and workshops suddenly (miraculously!) became accessible to us during Covid when nondisabled people needed access and online hosting became commonplace. Not only physically accessible, but often free or with pay-what-you-can options. For the first time, we were 'in the room' with other poetry folks. And, just as dramatically, so many events and poetry opportunities have disappeared as the rest of the world has 'gone back to normal.'

This lack of accessibility and inclusion in the poetry world is echoed in queer spaces and communities. These physical places are often in dark alleyways, dank basements, or up a rickety flight of stairs to the cheapest room in the attic. Centuries of us queer folks hiding in plain sight and things haven't changed all that much. And for a community that traditionally prizes physical looks and sexual performance, where do we bodywonky, neurospicy types fit in?

So we wanted to do more for this marginalised group within an already marginalised group, other than curate a hot collection of poetry about our sex lives. Thanks to funding from Arts Council England, we've been able to do just that. We've run free poetry workshops, online and open to all – shoutout to Sallyanne Rock and Gayathiri Kamalakanthan for delivering their brilliant sessions. We've offered mentoring sessions in poetry and performance to our contributors, thanks to the fabulous Éadaoín Lynch and Carrot, who've also provided support to us on this journey. And there's so much more to come (fnar fnar). We have a veritable box of erotic delights in the months ahead to promote this book on our *This Is Not A Sideshow* mini tour of the country. We've partnered with local queer disabled performers and groups to deliver poetry-cum-cabaret events in queer venues in as many nooks and crannies of the UK that funding, time, and our collective spoons would allow.

Along the way we've also had brilliant support from Susanna Clark from *Ingenious Fools* who helped us with our successful ACE application. JP received a small creative grant from Brave Words which helped cover some initial expenses before we received Arts Council funding. We sought advice from the activist artistic collective *Quiplash* and had wonderful support from the multi award-winning disability activist Andrew Gurza.

Access is sexy. So is activism. The LGBTQIA+ community has long reclaimed the word 'queer', used commonly as a slur up until the 1990s. Similarly, many members of the disabled and chronically ill community have reclaimed the term 'crip', and many with learning impairments or neurodivergence have reclaimed the word 'mad'. We want to honour these reclamations and the activist and anti-discrimination objectives of the *eff-able* project. We're conscious that not everyone is comfortable with these terms, and certainly not all contributors in this book will choose to use them. We made a deliberate decision not to assess a contributor's queerness or disability, allowing people to self-define. We have adopted the Social Model of Disability for this language, placing emphasis on *Disabled* people, as in people who may have a physical or mental impairment of some kind, disabled by an ableist society. As with the term 'queer', where you read 'disabled', this is a catch-all term, that not everyone in this book will wish to use to define their lived experience. It may encompass physical impairments, chronic illness, D/deaf people, those with autism, ADHD, or neurodivergence of any kind. Regardless of how individuals choose to define their sexuality or (dis)abilities, we are a community that deserves to be heard.

9

Hence: eff-able. Effable, meaning something that is capable of being uttered or expressed – our collective voices raised loud in anger and joy. And effable as in fuckable. The world may disable us or treat us as 'other', but the way in which we choose to give and receive pleasure (or choose not to) is entirely 'normal'.

When we opened for submissions, we had no idea what we'd get. Was it just us being Poetry Pervs after all, and *eff-able* some sort of wet dream? It was partly for this reason, and partly because we love their work so much that we secured the talents of our three Featured Poets. We're honoured and delighted to have the poetic pearls of UK slam champion Rick Dove, writer and disability activist Karl Knights, and award-winning poet and publisher Scarlett Ward. We received over 360 poems from 180 poets and could not be more delighted at their quality and diversity. It was a hard job narrowing it down to those chosen for the anthology, and we want to thank all those who submitted for sharing their words, and their lived experiences – it's been a joy and honour to read them all.

Huge thanks also to Janine Stromberg for her brilliant designs, and much gratitude and queer crip love to Ben Townley-Canning, without whom this book would not exist. When we thought about our ideal publisher for this anthology, there was only one name on our list: *fourteen poems*. We're thankful that Ben supported our crazy idea from the start, and it is with huge pride that we present the first ever (that we know of!) anthology of queer disabled poets writing about sex, body positivity, and erotic experience.

We're delighted to share with you 39 such effable nuggets – sexy poems, poignant poems, political poems; poems full of heartbreak, handjobs, and hotel rooms; respirators, callipers, and incontinence pads; masturbation, orgiastic joy, and a whole lot of kink. Us queer crip folk really do love our kink. We also have a whole range of poetic styles and forms, truly something for everyone, demonstrating what a diverse, exciting, and sexy a.f. community we are. This is the book we searched for, the one we wanted to read. May it also bring you joy, in whatever form you desire.

JP Seabright & George Violet Parker, London, March 2025

Fingering Elegy

When body had forgotten its purpose,
when hands curled up like swollen marmalade
cats refusing to move. When it couldn't
hold a fork. When I worried this was a wedge
between us. When it ate like a stray I was taming
from my palm. When doctors were obsessed
with it, and it spent hours inside a machine
wishing it was you scanning the pelvis for clues;
snatching the ghost mask off its white blood
cells. When I thought red hands too weak
to be a dyke, you bought it a strap on, reminded it
forks are merely formality. We slid into each other –
soft sliced bread in a toaster. Became hot and golden,
two crusty suns. We broke apart and clouds of steam
Edened the air around us. My heart hammered
like a police raid. And my body let it in.

I love men that have it brutal but make it gorgeous

I love men with sunken pecs.
I love men with more hair on their shoulders than their chest.
I love men with scars like two half moons meeting to kiss.
I love men that cry and cry and cry and then stop crying and can't cry.
I love men that don't have a dick.
I love men with dicks so big you can't even imagine because actually
the dick is a fist.
I love men that other men hate.
I love men whose beards look like the pubes of the face.
I love men that are sick and aren't getting better but still give great
head, weekly, at both the bathhouse and the dyke bar bathroom.
I love men with bad style, clothes that don't fit because the body's
changed too fast and the next SSI payment hasn't come through.
I love men who just got out of inpatient and are annoying their
friends.
I love men that sweat too much.
I love men that smell like second puberty and can't quite figure out
how to mask it.
I love men that can't quite figure out how to make money but still use their
food stamps money to buy their boyfriend the cutest medium-priced flowers
from Trader Joe's every month.
I love men that used to be dykes and dykes that are also men and
fags that are almost men and not quite women.
I love bisexual men that say "I have a girlfriend" but no-one believes
them because they are so "effeminate".
I love men that are shameless.
I love men that are learning to name their feelings.

I love men that are average artists and average athletes and don't really care that they are average.

I love men with too many long-distance girlfriends.

I love men that are therapists, baristas, DEI consultants and micro-influencers for the cash.

I love men that squirt.

I love men that shave their pussy while looking in a hand mirror.

And more than anything – I love men that move with grace even when the world wants them flatlined, laying on the pavement like stinky roadkill in the heat of summer whimpering "I hate myself" over and over and over again.

ELSPETH WILSON

Sick days as tiny revolutions

Groggy dozing, you fetching me
decaffeinated tea, stumbling
to the shower, the dog jumping
up to say she loves me. More
snoozing. Until – your lunch break.
You slide in, next to me, your hands
playing where there's pain and weariness
but oh so much else besides; a wanting
that roots around you, giggles
as your stubble exfoliates my unwashed
skin. Dirty and delighted with it.
Two bodies that don't fit, fitting
together, snatched minutes of sheer
focus as your tongue dances
with mine, then moves down, down, down
            worshipping the parts of me
that I fight every day to love.
Knowing that we are gorgeous,
we are glowing, we are shuffling,
we are sick. We are so, so – Fuck
everything that says we are not those
things, fuck work, fuck productivity,
fuck me. Wrap those things together
and let's give each other the best
orgasms of our life, babe, yes,
don't go back to work, no, don't answer
that email, let's come
together and destroy

Job Centres, means-testing,
the way your mum flinches when I say
disabled, the whole lot, yes, yes, yes (!)
            yes, babe, yes, exactly there.

Mad Love Manifesto

I've savoured sweat-sodden glide under pulses of light. Been
contraption of muscle and filthy intent. Slapped and grabbed and spat
and scratched, concealed myself in bricolage of hands. After, been
kissed and not kissed. I've been glad tangle, reluctant arch, lethargic
sprawl. Learned beyond too much, there's more. Been six
inches of silicone and tomorrow's welcome ache. Admired pianist's
fingers sinking into arias. Sucked each note off his knuckles later.
Shucked secrets. Twinned tongues. Been pliant as a thumb plunged
into candle wax. Made clowns, psychics, and scholars fall to their
knees. Staged a mutiny, sharpened an excuse. Let my body be
someone else's problem for the night. Crushed promises as soft suds
into dark brambles of hair. I've dashed myself against sleazy lines.
Fashioned clichés from red lace and cheap hotels. Been riptide and
ricochet, petrol slick to blaze. Exasperated, troubled, and capsized.
Refused to be anybody else's delight. Cried. Feared I'd exhausted a
limitless supply. Resurrected myself in myth and gold. Held sacred.
Smouldered. Felt orifice derive from both mouth and make. Slipped
oysters down my throat. Welcomed raindrops on my upturned face.
Spent Sundays under freckled kisses and chestnut blight. Felt cold
brick and stilled currents at my back. I've sullied bath water and spring
water and my own holy no. Claimed every last gaspful of it as
my own. I've felt moonlight spill over soil. Been swagger and a sure
hand pushing deeper. Been sheet-stain and neighbour mither.
Laughed together in the shower after.

Inside

"this places endometriosis at the extreme end of diagnostic inefficiency"
– Wikipedia

it is when i am on my knees
i remember there is a limit
to what skin can tell you
also blood   even spit

these are things you can leave behind

on an inner thigh   on a cinema seat
smeared on the ten of a pain scale
the red of a traffic light system

within the pink-slapped cold
of a bedsit flat   of a glass of water
burns the thrumming coals of
a hundred soft-tongued questions

how much   how long   who for

two or three fingers
pushing at the door to peek
to listen

the only way to know
to really really know
is in

What Gay Porn Doesn't Show

The ultimate tease, the three-hour bus trip
give or take thirty minutes, to his front door.
I want him like that, plodding, tractor slow.
No showy moves, my legs round his waist.
Pillows beneath my tailbone, cold side up.
Waiting out a spasm, he brings belly pudge
to my chapped lips. I snog overalls, petrol
days spent under land rovers. A giggle break
for the thrusting parp noises we can't help.
His hot wheezy chuckle on my shoulder.
When Mum texted 'don't come back'
it was this warm duvet hush she wanted
rid of. Or was it him growing inside me
like a gulped Granny Smith seed?
*

I wasn't told hook-ups could be like this.
Tom's fingers in front of the electric heater
before we start physio, on the mat he snagged
for me, lent by his gran, at the foot of the bed.
His right wrist, in the shadow behind my knee.
The way to my iffy heart is chock fulla questions.
'How was it last night?' 'Am I stretching too far?'
His gloved hands, my grab bar into the shower.
He squirts Poundland shampoo over my palm.
I didn't know want would arrive in Wrentham
like a pigeon perching on a scarecrow's arm.
A Tupperware salad, my name in his marker.
A peck before the only morning bus pulls in
a knobble of sugar beet between my teeth.

Divergent Flesh

Before you said, *Can I?*
I hadn't imagined
you would want to open
my incontinence pad,
go down on me.
I hadn't seen my Spina Bifida body
as anything but medicalised,
the bang-up job a young surgeon
runs home and tells his wife about:
I saved a woman's life today.
Hadn't seen my body as anything but
married: shoehorned
into the one-flesh-fits-all rule
of straight, right-bodied matrimony,
the sunken cost of oath and duty.
Only after the bread is broken
can the tender inside be enjoyed.
It never happened again the same way
but I'm still sunken, differently. Under you
I know I am no burden.
I am something taken up, both eyes open,
fingers clasped shut. You remind me
I am not the patent pending of men; that I need
to unlearn the tyranny of needing
to refrain from asking for anything unsanitary
to be done to me, just for the fuck
sake of it, because my skin is yearning;
that, fellatio reassigned to memory,
I can still be under you now, begging

21

you to keep me under you,
not as a student, learning
under a sensei; or a waiting list, creaking
under a mismanaged NHS; but as grass
under a drifting catkin,
finding enough new inches
with which to rise and meet it.
Before you said, *Can I?*
I scarcely imagined
I could say, *You may.*

Bright orange hoodie from Tesco

it waited for you, reduced
to eye it up
you teased it at first,
held it
in both hands,
looked it up
and down, caressed it,
imagined it on me,
imagined your hands on it
on me
fingered the inside
to see how soft it was
and then

      put it back

you knew
that when it was twice reduced
I'd love it twice
as much, find
kinship in   continued rejection,
the waiting,
longing,
crying out
you

remembered
how the colour   was drained

out of my life,   the softness
I was told I didn't like,   withheld,
everything baggy
to hide
(my body)
and this hoodie, a medium
fits perfectly,
slides   perfectly
off
when you undress me

this isn't
really a poem
about a hoodie,
it's a poem about the way
everything
                              you touch
that I touch
makes love to me

how I'm reduced
to softness
in your hands

Invocation

meet me where the river becomes   a mouth
where grass trails from the lip   like ribbons of skin torn
by my teeth teeth teeth   come where the water is
blackest   where I finger the abyss widdershins and long
for a mouth   to close around the digit
telescope goldfish all eyes   and barracuda innocence

part the water like a veil   and rise
my bride white as an eyeball   spite the dark
a sodden laced curtain clings   to your perpetual gasp
lips thick like a riverbank   you draw nearer my Magritte lover
mirror our lips   guppy open sharing humid breaths

cleanse me like the doctor fish   stretch this moment
like wet cotton do not go   do not go
sucked below the surface   I am alone on the bank
panting tulle clouds   fists full of damp earth
condensed   by morning I go home
lie in the bath   kiss bedsheets under clouds of steam.

An ode to salt

Before the tequila,
all sea and no sour.
You draw patterns in the snowflakes
of the restaurant table of my back.
Take the pot
circle my body
a ritual. All that is sacred
ends with an O.

Bathe me in it, rough
gravel against my skin.

When my doctor tells me
to increase my intake.
I devour the tidal wave
of your neck.

Dip my tongue
into your soft flesh.

You put your fingers
in my mouth
after screwing
back on the lid
of the pickle jar.

I taste you
every time I season
my chips.

the moon &

Love is abundant – but you grew up
amid Black Friday sales and cryptocurrency,
psychiatric wards like prisons, prisons like
prisons, streets like labyrinths and marble runs,
everyone hurrying down and down separately,
inexplicable heterosexualism, the stock market,
empty buildings on High Street. Whisper gently
to your skin, which is a lover grown aloof. Go out
under the moon & feel how much she yearns for you
(mostly water), her heavy brass body full of desire.
You're sure there's a trick, some sleight of hand
will transform the lovely curls beneath your fingers into air
when you tilt your boyfriend's face towards yours
and his eyes are as vast & weightless blue as the moon.
That everything you have ever loved is secretly numbers
whirring on a server halfway across the world,
that sex is spoken behind closed doors
in an impossible language, that your disabled bed
is a raft drifting out on a calm ocean and the
breeze from your window is full of salt and sunlight.
If you close your eyes you can almost feel
the specks of sea spray lightly on your face.
When you stand on the picket line chanting you begin
to share voices with everyone around you & a heart.
You speak with a strange voice into a megaphone
and the winter street echoes it back to you. One day
you will connect with everything. You will be
the heavy moon at your centre &
the thousand eyes gazing up at her.

Pharmakon

Darling,
I love the way you slice open
blisterpacks, with a deft fingernail.
How my two-tone pill dissolves
beneath your palm's heat.
You hold it to your nose, inhale.
This one smells of elderberry and dust
you say, as you place it on my tongue.
I roll it round my mouth,
tease its softening crust,
let it wash down, cool, endured.
It tastes of cinnamon and lust.

You pass my white pill mouth-to-mouth,
controlled substance dancing on our lips,
our lipsticks mingle, leave a blackberry stain.
I have a good half hour, I say,
before that kicks in.
I shift my hips so they align with yours,
our breasts brush, we savour skin on skin
and wait until the edge falls off my pain.

Your fingertips play with a pair
of pert, blue pills.
You pinch them into me,
devour, swallow, ingest,
taste their sickroom scent
of camphor oil, and lemon zest.

What's this one? You say
as you hold it to the light,
tiny as a harvest moon.
I stay your hand;
Later, I say, *it's far too soon,*
I'll fall asleep.
I pull you to me, taste familiarity,
moonbeams and a dulcet sea,
lie back and think of pharmakon,
let you love each pill-filled part of me.

Body flares, consumes, digests,
tablets fizz, dissolve inside,
a tide of side-effects explodes
like distant stars, expand, collide.

Afterwards, you don't forget,
fetch fresh water, feed me the moon,
let me slowly numb and drift,
dim the light and stroke my head,
place the bottles by my bed,
a gift.

inhaler as foreplay

I joke, but it's pavlovian
twist your inhaler, two quick puffs
clothes off, no romance now
not with two children & only these
snapshot speed moments –
your taut tight body, mine
softer, riper, a damn sight tireder
but fuck – I still want you as hard
as I did 17 years ago, our one night,
that afternoon delight, you – a boy of 17
me – older than you, not wiser. I fucked
then to know I was alive, human.
fucking to feel something, letting
my body be there, just an object
just a moment. now –

I know myself. know that I am loved,
that I am me, whore and madonna,
not defined by breasts or cunt, not
just a warm body. we kiss,
fierce & quick against the clock,
against the knock on the door, grinding
down on your beautiful cock. your mouth
whispers breathlessly I love you,
my body tells you
oh god
me too

Unanswered questions for household items

I sometimes wonder if my stick knows we are fucking,
if the handrails on my bathroom wall regard me as sexual.
I think of the proximity between my perching stool and cunt
and wonder if it ever inhales me, enjoys my scent
as I stir peppers, onions –
my steel bed rail has seen some things:
I would love to ask it how my scars appear when I am prostrate,
whether my arsehole looks edible.
I wonder if my bedside table loves to hear me orgasm,
soaking up heavy breaths, me, not letting up until I'm hoarse.
And I ask you, repeatedly, if you can accommodate my hips,
worry deeply that the fact I can't always wrap my thighs around your
naked form
will make you want to leave me; my brain is full
of heroin-chic-hardbodies-Mad-Lizzie-fitness
expectations of the 80s
and disability has made me soft around my edges.
I shouldn't worry, though. Because you seem to love the way I
compensate for rusted hips
by sitting on your needy lips, our sofa arm a crutch
and you drink me like orange juice –
later, you will fuck me, right over it,
and my legs will buckle for different reasons.
I wonder if this sofa loves the role it plays in these epic escapades,
And if it shares squalid stories with the windowsill
about the times it's felt my naked breasts pressed hard against it,
or if it offers war stories to the pillows
of being sprayed with your cum.

ELENA SICHROVSKY

This Rug Is Not For Masturbating

that's what it said on the sign in the store window
okay then why does the rug look like every dick
ive ever sucked why does it look like every dyke
ive ever fucked why does it look like every deer
ive ever lucked out of hitting not for lack of trying

to destroy something beautiful like a body or a rug
is to take away its power to destroy you first
is to call your wounds trophies and not scars
is to have a story to tell at company dinners

here is the time i rubbed all my depression out
on a rug in the furniture store and the shop attendants
cheered me on and some said i did it for clout
of course it was i only get out of bed for an audience

i get banned from the store, okay
i trend on twitter all week, okay
i get a uti and antibiotics, okay
i try to kill myself with, okay, a safety pin

where did u get that from says the doctor
the rug i say /which rug/ well the rug
gyrating on your office floor

The Status Quo Is God

Huckleberry, hog jowls or bad apple—there is always a pie cooling on a windowsill. This poem is only tangentially about schizophrenia.

Insanity is doing the same thing over and over is a comphet adage. I survived The Tens on Nickelodeon and an undeclared crush on you.

I like how you sit ever so still on a barstool, and at the movies, unflinching during the jump scares. A human furniture fetish is a tough subject to broach.

A perverse aroma morphs into a pair of diaphanous hands. Good pet, good ghost, good gag, good lard, good stink—it sweeps the hungry off our feet.

Next to you, I stir like an endless slurry of wet gravel under the back tires of a crashed Tesla. Fidgeting is a symptom. So are repetitive behaviours.

Tomorrow, I might walk in sure and untrammelled circles. The day after, I'll arrange myself into a life form that can exist in your bed.

This poem predicts the future more accurately than acid reflux. Stone fruit mouthful. Or meringue. Or molasses. Even my oesophagus is hot for you.

If I talk to god, I'm praying. If god talks to me, something's up with my meds. You and I? Well, we've had the same conversation about honest fear for years.

Slapstick. It's a classic bit—in order to steal the pie from the windowsill, our hero must outsmart the bulldog, baboon or rabid gravity that guards it. Whenever you wear those chelsea boots, I fantasise of holding the left one over my mouth like an anaesthesia mask and counting backward from ten. By the end of the episode wounded cartoons are always perfectly fine. With you, I want to abandon all notions that separate body from sound,

that separate buttercrust from time, separate watchdogs from existential crisis arousal from animation. Did you hear a whistle pitch when we finally kissed?

Paradise in the catacombs

Praise the sex
bench nestled in the concrete
cathedral of confessionary shadows
conspiring in the queer rave playroom.

Praise its nuts and bolts
sturdy and proud as my joints are taken
to their limits of extension as I rail
at the concave heavens, prophetic, profane. Praying. Taking
Jesus' name. Praise

to the bench for its perfect height,
padded leather just right.
Its bars girthy enough to withstand ecstatic rites,
fast-closing fists, bucking hips,
ricocheting praise off benevolent bricked walls. Submit

to every indulgent whim. We'll whip
up a zealot's prayer. I'll speak in tongues,
crucify your pain on my supplicant face.

Praise gloaming domes that arch
like orgasming spine
above our feast piteous, pious, perverse.
Take a peek under God's skirts. Baptise the dirt.
Press novice palms to mattress. Vanish. Steady the earth.
Prostrate your need. Expose
the delicate skin of the soles of your feet. Brace.

                              Communion partners multiply
                              like baskets of bread
                              passed around.

Praise this holy ground, these sacrosanct rituals.
In the dark, on all fours, walking stick leant against mirrored wall,
you can't tell: God missed a spot.

Bog Body

The body at war with itself. Desire as a hollowed-out shell, a carcass sun-bleached and thirsty. Time as a killer of dreams. The future erased. Nothing looping back in on itself. An infinity of bones. Hello, cruel world. My body as the thing no one wants to talk about. The hushed murmurs. The sideways glances. Hello, dirt eater. The soil as food for the dead, nutrient-rich and earthy. I count myself among them. The never havers. The empty souled. I visit the burial ground every evening. Pull the grass and gravel over my head. Hold my breath for as long as I can. The body as a hospital with no doctors. The body as a scalpel carving into the overgrowth. I become nobody so quickly. Replaceable. Forgettable. Undesirable. Hello, spiraling thoughts. Welcome to my home. Take your shoes off at the door. Here is the bed. Here is a tongue. Here is a fantasy replayed for your viewing pleasure. The body is disgusting. The body is foul. The body is a prison cell overflowing with sewage and cockroaches and flies and scabies. Hello, object of desire. Welcome to the dirty and the reviled. Love as a burst eardrum, the constant ringing and I can't hear a damn thing else. Love as an intestine bleeding and desperate to be mutilated. Love as the bright red toilet water. Love as every lonely night spent imagining a body that doesn't hurt itself. Love as shame. The limitations of what I can never be. Every failing. Every shortcoming. Every regret. Every short-sighted confession and heartbreak deferred. I went searching for a river in an endless cavern. When I stumbled upon its banks in the dark, damp cave, I wanted to drink all of its water and so I did. I consumed an ecosystem and made an aquarium of my body. It wasn't long before the nausea kicked in. How cruel it is for that which gives us life to also be a poison. I laid down in the hollowed-out riverbed and waited for the end. I imagined my carcass preserved like a bog body, all mummified skin and sopping wet. I became sad that no one would get to see my bones. I have such a pretty skeleton, underneath it all.

Pain/Vein

Open the poppy veil
    blood vein

                outside the damp skin

    flow water crystals
        over the blue vein

queer this touch gentle outside the blood line

  memory crystal outside the vein blood stutter shutter door
        thud blood cry lithium metal mood

    morphine dimmer plant elder

    plant archive of opium poppy latex
        dry this ink

         to scry the vein to score the pain deep to the bed

    veil blood metal asylum

spoon bangs the walls pans plate

    bars clang in material history

    bio stone alchemy in the blood

vibrational memory lines
         dissect asylum

open the vein

    shelter the poppy mood sap tired so low

       vein bangs DNA resonance

scorch the blood
    line to metal bar the wall metal salt

crystal resonate shelter asylum shelter smelt

dried bed river red bed vein
your tender
ancestral touch

Chirp Chirp

The story's old:
                    we fall in love and head
like geckos across the ceiling.
                            We uncover
a garden of mirth, a dragonfly baubled with dew
that's a flying Christmas tree.
                            Your hearing aid
makes a sound like crickets.
                        Even so,
I've lived in a hydrangea before.
The sky was blue petals and all my friends
were aphids
            but I couldn't stay there.
I watched small windmills of suspicion turn
and wound up lonely.
                    Let's keep things crooked
for now.
            Let's fit together like question marks.
I won't ask who you are
                        but I'll listen
each evening to what the crickets tell me.

KATIE (TOM) WALTERS

Give me a column in the telegraph and I will write about moss

how the sweet stuff knows nothing of violence.
how it's possible to be both immutable
and tender; that the smallest of tendrils can
take root in stone. this may be tough to understand, but i have felt
the warmth between our bodies and i know how very far we are
from dying. peel moss from the wall, and it lives,
it still lives. such a soft and feathered thing.
growing where it ought not grow, making pillows
out of concrete. let us feel them, cool and yielding
underneath us. the night sky is a transsexual.
she tells me this repeatedly, as we fuck in her holiest hour and
unsightly plants spread slick in the dark, going nowhere, going
nowhere else but here.

The Erotics of Crip Time // Lessons in Flower Pressing

Let me teach you to be
slow, that desire
only
strengthens
at softer tempos –
let me teach you
about feeling weak,
giving into something
(someone), relinquishing
control,
let me teach you about
the erotics of a body
finding itself
in its own
folds, in quiet
moments, in tiny
moments, in
time

Let me show you
what it means to be
embodied, to
know your borders and
know that you exceed
them, to come
back to yourself,
in all your

messy physicality,
again and again and
let me touch you –
trace a line around your
edges; the rounding
of your nose, your hips
commas, pausing between
halves, the scars
across your chest semi-
circular
growth
rings

Let us hold each
other, press our hearts
together, two
pansies between pages,
let us remember our
pleasure is timebending,
an act of resistance;
let us be still, here
for a while,
ink stains on paper
broken and beautiful and
refusing to
wither

Puberty cookies

Dough sticks between our fingers
as we knead on tables
in the chadar ochel. We shape balls
and tits, a long tube for a penis,
a triangular shape for a vagina.

We make marshmallow clits,
place chocolate chips in the centre
of dough circles for nipples.
Scatter sprinkles for pubes. We laugh,
hold up trays with our creations.

Our counsellors take the lumpy dough
into the kitchen, pop it in the oven.
It transforms:
balls mashed into penises,
rhomboid-shaped vaginas.

We devour our cookie bodies,
savour them, as ugly
and misshapen as could be.

There's no cure, but kink helps

For Ori

Me: Part-time boi   full-time faggot.
You: Coquettishly   kissable with chap-
stick lips and upper lip face fuzz.

My spine's click   echoes the room
as I pounce on you. You giggle, I giggle.
You make me feel. You make me

and unmake me. You make me:
      hard   wet   horny   hot   sexy   sensual   sapphic.

You make me:
      gay   queer   T4T   faggy   fucky   genderfucky   gender-bent
      out of shape   then right back into shape   again.

You make me feel:
      undeniably understood   useful   good   wanted   filled and full-
      y alive. Even when my hand cramps inside you. Even when my neck
      pop-cracks as I push my head forward, my lips tracing the tip
                  of your cock.

You giggle, I giggle.
You break, I break.
I feel less broken
with you.

After the Adult Disability Payment Tribunal

After the Adult Disability Payment Tribunal we
got into bed and laid our bodies
delicately together – two spoons
cupped in each other's curves, my
buoyant arse against the bottom
of your soft, rounded belly, your
arms across the arc of my breasts, my
back resting against the breadth
of your chest my neck nestled
against the kiss of your warm mouth
your nose burrowed in the shower
fresh bouquet of my hair, together
using our breath to reset our
adrenaline-flooded nervous systems.
Making our bodies safe
again. Sheltering from the quiet
violence of a precarious future

When Google returns five million four hundred eighty thousand results for fucking

I know we aren't there
in these bodies of uncountable nouns
come here
take your clothes off
there's enough gender to go round
for the way we enter
each other as in ourselves
as in today the clouds are a heavy colour on our heads
and the sun is an alarming shade of blonde
and you taste better than power
falling like pedantic light across every naked adverb
in which you held my cock on your tongue
as I ate out all the signified parts of you
and you taste better without recourse to colonial gender
in pain for the parts of desire
similarly ejected
pitched into the societal overboard
where archive is
made is out
as what was always
bound to happen
my body
dear
desirous
extractively abandoned
I will be as crip
as queer as I am

yet we who are born in the claim and residence
of queerness and criphood
melt our words apart
in the history before
the securitisation of medicine
and the national body at stake
as we know of it now
comes a time when we are all enthusiasm
parts equally penetrable
in which you fill yourself
inside up for me
release other ways to be with me
Hot To Go for me
I want to grasp your name
as a verb
in the vowels of my mouth
till time approaches dilation
o hold me in this place
of desire-wracked sonancy
let me circlude you
in the palace of my flesh
its very agony
opening in love
I promise I want you
I promise
I'll meet you there

A benediction for want

God cast out the gentle weight of this   urge
to compulsively check your phone for throbbing heart pixels
losing yourself   in the pulse of a surname.

We are all of us tethered to this earth by tiny aches.
So much of a body is part prayer   part ruin.
The body cannot sit still in its own undoing.
God entreat your marrow to still in its tsunami,
soften the suck of tide before the swell.

[
Not content in scattering anymore, lately I mist.
        When I tell you
        I am wet
        please believe
        that I am rainfall

        for all the world,
        a tree-canopy deluge
        bowing the fingertip
        fronds of fern.
]

Let not your Venn diagram circles
'Pain'   and   'Desire'
align in their shape like planets.

Like pain, want does not knock and wait to be allowed in
it simply eclipses everything   leaks into tender flesh   and hollow
places

as though learning to shape itself   into the soft palate.
May you never mind the urgency
and find it wonting.

[

      I am hungry the way a comma is always
        hungry,   expectant of breath,   always,
I am dying to know what mercies your body allows you before it
breaks.
                    Some days my breaking comes
              unpredicted,
                  others I prepare a place for it at the
                  table.
I would devour you like that;
intricately planned   and intentional.
I no longer ask for mercy from blood test alchemy or neurology,
but I would get on my knees for you.
                  I don't need you
                  to tell me I take too much
                  my neurons often gossip that of me
                  as they dissolve
                  under my blood's fine chisel.

]

May you sit in the paper skin of all this   want
humming in the relentlessness   of clocks
letting it fold you   into the shape   of a request.

Fulcrum

I
will
define
it: pivot-point
reckon   ing   line-
break   volta   it's   when
you and me   merge   breath
to   breath   dysphoria   overcome
by trust   by presence   how i see   now
beauty   in what   my body   can do
how it feels   when it is   the right   person
doing   the   feeling.

manifesto

how about you go on top this time. how about you fuck me to morning. while i lie here and watch. how about you ride me like a cockhorse. your ring on my finger. your cunt in my mouth. i divide like the red sea. all that is holy is profane. all that is solid melts into air. all that is me is under your thumb.

how about i stop asking questions. kiss you right there right now. hard on your soft lips that drip into mine. how about you break me open. while i make you cry out. my jaw dancing joy on your pelvic bone. lactic burns to the sound of your moans. your body a flower blooming. petals flame as you come.

how about we take time for a breather. a snack. a nap. and a litre of water. how about i hold on to the side of the bed. head spun with vertigo. corkscrewing inside you. let's turn all the lights off. it's too much. i'm flooding. falling from you. i'm crashing this party. desire overload. fuck me. fuck ME. fuck.

journal (take #26)

dear diary, for a while every time i got a uti after sex with a man, he was from long island and i thought something was seriously wrong with the place. diary, if my sex life of yore were a book, it would be a series of unfortunate events—first of all, i didn't cum till i was twenty-one and fucking a couple (complete by her hand), then didn't realize it until i bought the right vibrator two years later, taught myself to finish with forbidden mental footage and r/sluttyconfessions. imagine my surprise when, having repeated my success with others exactly twice while drunk or high, he lets me use him like a toy and i explode in minutes. dear diary, who could blame my hunger as i slip desperate fingers into, across swollen lips, buck hips up and down on goldilocks length—*juuuuust right* by way of *riiiight there*—with a slick of shared fluids shining in the bisexual blue and pink of the lamplight. this is vonnegut's hawk with velvet claws: the exact shape of how i want to be adored.

fucked

to be	a spine	biting
ice	blue	to be pain
lingering	lingering	lingering
she can't name	the body	in her bed
now	thoroughly fucked	having only met
the night before	& yet	here
they are	faces smudged	willing
emptied of things	like shame	ooze
that ooze	& gunk	& muck
but yes! again	they are	both exactly here
slurping	clutching	lapping
bodies of glass	hot & glittering	brittle with morning

Portrait of Madame X

after John Singer Sargent

If it were I, in the black satin gown,
raised above every woman in the room,
the one with the pale skin you like so much,
a shoulder chain dropped, too scandalous,
he'll repaint it in a less provocative place,
corseted in velvet, a wasp, that pinched waist,
enthralled in gold, framed, untouched,
my cold flesh in opposition to my sex's sin.
You'd ask me to take off my dark clothes.
A spotlight on my pearlescent neck exposes
me for what I really am, the body as pure sex.
By which you'd mean, I am to be possessed.
Gaze at my shoulders—watch me unrobe.
Classical you say, touching only yourself.

sex with a smashed femoral head

i stashed gladioli
in my cunt

watered
my dead
hip deader

tried to fuck you
upended by pain

osteoarthritis
riddling me
into riddles

where are you?
bold one
the one that screams in my head

where are you?
the one
who i'd
do over

black and blue

come round please
blow my flowers

feel all the stamens
stick
to your
cheek

i want you
like this

splayed out on my bed
sucking my petals

the pain is so deep

"end stage"
says the nhs x ray
end stage
of my
hissing hip

i don't know
if i can finish you off

but let me take pain killers
and rip into
you

plague
you
with pollen

before the surgeon
fills me
with ceramic
and polyethylene

bequeaths me
a fresh leg
and
a good stick

Nail

; ;
/

Nail
I want you   in my bed.   ; ;
I want you   inside   my walls   ; ;   /
of keratin,   hiking up   the skirt   /
of my cuticle, penetrating   under my
skin. I want   you   in my   bloodstream.
I want to   be sick   off you, my   blood cells in   ; ;
body to body   combat   with   you.   I want   /
to be sick of you;   I   want   to vomit   you
like the tail end   of a   bad dream,   garbled,   ; ;
embracing   porcelain   fervently,   heaving   /
until my   stomach   bottoms out   like my
coin purse   overturned,   its silk lining:
a vacancy, waiting   to be filled. I want
every   downy   hair   plucked   ; ;
off   my body   assembled into   /
a visage of you–
of you
blown
by lips,
by wind.
you are
not a   ; ;
dandelion,   /
I know.
I'm not
sure
I can sleep
this off.

best-laid plans

Despite careful pre-
planning (wheelchair
accessible room – check!
– king-size bed – check!)
yet another hotel room
yields two single beds.

Our precious fucking time
thwarted. Our bodies
infantalised by your twisted,
normie gaze. Feral want
rendered chaste by lack
of imagination: crips

can't possibly have sex – No
hospitality for us. I wait
in the lobby, by the uncomfortable
vinyl chairs, my walking stick poised
and angled – Chaplin-esque,
in sympatico with the silent comedy

enfolding as you have a stand-off
with the reception staff, the metal
yellow go faster stripes
on your wheelchair glinting
with your righteous irritation.
Eventually another, more suitable

room is offered. You accept but try
to push for a discount. A fair exchange
for the daily inconvenience and discrimination
No? Come on now! Listen,
we will brazenly exploit your discomfort
and flicker of shame. This is the dance –

We make you feel better with our
banter as you go through the empty
health-and-safety-in-the-event
-of-a-fire spiel but let's get real,
we all fucking know that in truth
should this building catch alight

we would be the very last thing
                    on your mind

Choke Me With My Sunflower Lanyard

Choke me here, on the living room carpet,
watching TV. Sunflower ribbon against
hyoid as your thumbs press the veins of my
neck. Kneeling on burning knees, I can't
stutter, can't speak. You force me to gaze
into your eyes, the greatest intimacy of all,
as my pulse thins and blurs to nothing. Then
you let go: I fall forward between your
thighs, gasp in the sweet metal of your
vulva. You collared me in this green lanyard,
you wrote your name as my in-case-of-
emergency: nothing is so romantic. All day,
my too-keen nose is sickened by pine-
scented air fresheners, post-gym bananas,
migraine-buzz of candle smoke, but it's
worth it when I find the musk of your groin.
My mouth waters. I bury my face in you, a
mole seeking tender roots, lick my way to
your centre. I'm your creature, I have a
place.

Halo

Some facts for the record about my observable universe:
Sometimes a moment, under excitation, can dilate
enough for its edges to disappear from view,
The ends of fingers, the beginnings of you,
skin glistening,
         skin flushing,
                skin fusing,
and sticking to skin,
sinews beyond the reach of perception, becoming
lost inside each other, as the Gateway Theory of Pain
dictates the brain can only process the singular
brightest sensation, like trying to see stars
beyond the midday sun.
How a mouth can swallow anything,
when it is opened wide enough,
but how still, in these constant incursions expanding,
the Pauli Exclusion Principle means
we remain two people, even as the evidence of otherwise
mounts up, even as the evidence of edges passes
beyond our horizon, as this fusion generates its release
obscuring everything else, obscuring position and direction
Lost inside each other
thoughts collect like dust, invisible
until they settle, a nebula upon my shoulder,
an accretion disk caught in a flesh negative,
a ring of inaudible screams, forming red-shifted dreams,
Biting

I can never remember when it happens
But there, in the aftermath, the entirety
of the heavens as the light catches up,
I see where you sunk your teeth,
see stars beyond the midday sun,
see stars, the moment we were one,
a glimpse of forever,
drawn blood.

ARDEN FITZROY

To the Performer Hesitating in the Wings

If you ever drained a bottle
of champagne to toast
someone else's success ever
slammed into a glass door
full-force wearing a crop top
with a stomach full of vitriol
chain-smoked two packs before
having disappointing sex
with your nemesis
if you ever forgot your
lines while improvising
then stole a man's face
while he was still inside you
if you tethered yourself to a mast
when you needed to explode
let the splinters rot outwards
abandoned the pieces as a problem
for someone kinder to solve if you
ever had to save your own life
by destroying another's
stayed in your dressing gown
all day dreaming of the lives
of others escaped imprisonment by
hacking the key out of yourself got to
the end only to discover that you were
the punchline all along

take a bow.

Salt pig

This year made wild animals of us
afraid and mouth-foaming

phantom hand in the night
takes the brain, holds hard

sweating through sheets,
body aches, bad desire

I became the fever
wide-eyed   ravenous

hot as a july fuck

my tongue
curls back

and this mouth opens

to a perfect O

POET BIOS

POET BIOS

Amber Dawn lives on Coast Salish Territories (Vancouver, Canada). She's authored two novels, *Sub Rosa* and *Sodom Road Exit*; three poetry collections, and *How Poetry Saved My Life: A Hustler's Memoir.*

Arden Fitzroy is a writer-poet, actor, fighter, and producer. They believe in experimentation and blurring the boundaries of genre, gender, and art forms. Instagram/Bluesky: @ArdenFitzroy

Arlo Kean is a writer/creative based in East London. Their work has been published with T'ART Press and *Ink Sweat and Tears.*

Ben Dalitz is a poet, artist, and campaigner. Their work has been published in *Bi+ Lines: An Anthology of Contemporary Bi+ Poets* and Issue 12 of *fourteen poems.* When they write and dream queer liberation, they do so in deep solidarity with the people of Palestine.

Cat Chong is a poet, essayist, and publisher who completed their PhD at NTU, Singapore in 2024. Their work considers the intersections between gender, genre, and disability in experimental poetics.

Catherine Balaq is a writer and psychotherapist. She is co-editor of Black Cat Press. Her debut collection, *animaginary,* was published in 2023. *Deathless,* her second collection, was published in 2024. Catherine also writes novels.

Chloë Clarke is a queer, disabled poet. They are the former Young Poet Laureate of Worcestershire and currently live in London with their partner and silly sausage of a dog.

Claire Sosienski Smith is a neurodivergent poet based in Deptford, London. Their work has appeared in *Prolit, Porridge,* and Bell Press, and they are part of Resonance Poetry Collective.

Cleo Henry (they/them) is a London-based poet with an interest in queerness, giant squid, and the apocalypse. They released their first pamphlet, *The Last Lesbian Bar in the Midlands,* with *fourteen poems.* They have also been published in *Ambit* and *Selkie,* and by Banshee Press, Cipher Press, Pilot Press, and Broken Sleep Books.

Deviji RM Jaani-Jaan is a shape-shifting, multi-armed, QTIPOC, effable Goddess, frequently found fully prepared for any sensual delight: clutching lube, a hitachi magic wand, radar key, cbd gummies, a flask of empress grey tea, a hot water bottle, and a yummy vegan protein-filled snack. They also write, make film, art, and mischief. @devijijaan

Dylan McNulty-Holmes is the author of *Survivalism for Hedonists* (Querencia Press, 2023) and *Half a Million Mothers* (shortlisted for the 2022 New Media Writing Prize). More at dylanmcnultyholmes.com.

Elena Sichrovsky (she/they/it) is a queer disabled writer with a profound love for body horror. Their debut chapbook *Eating Out Anne Sexton* was released with Ghost City Press in 2024.

Elspeth Wilson is a Scottish writer and poet. She is the author of *Too Hot to Sleep* (Written Off Publishing, 2023) and *These Mortal Bodies* (Simon and Schuster, 2025).

Gayathiri Kamalakanthan is a Tamil poet and performer. They won the Disabled Poets Prize 2024 and their novel-in-verse, *Bad Queer,* is forthcoming with Faber. gayathiri.co.uk Instagram/Bluesky: @unembarrassable

George Violet Parker is a Pushcart, Best of the Net, and Space Crone Prize-nominated queer disabled writer, performer, co-op founder, and facilitator.

Publications include collaborative pamphlet *Not Your Orlando* (Punk Dust), *Twisted Roots* (Reconnecting Rainbows), and their debut collection *Gynandromorph* (Written Off). Other publications include *Mslexia, Financial Times, Arachne Press, Bi+ Lines,* and more.

Idony Lewis is a queer-crip poet and short fiction writer dwelling in the North. Their writing has been published by *Queer Bodies* (Broken Sleep Books), *The Poetry Business, A Velvet Giant, The Remote Body,* and many others.

Jackson Phoenix Nash (he/him) is a queer trans poet from Essex. His debut pamphlet, *Some People are Trains,* was published by Little Betty in 2024.

Jem Henderson is a genderqueer poet from Leeds. *an othered mother* and their collaborative project *GenderFux* came out in 2022 and *MotherFlux,* its sequel in 2024. A collection with Chris Cambell, *small plates,* is out now.

Jessica Whyte is a queer, disabled/neurodivergent writer and artist from East Sussex, with poems previously published by Paper Swans Press and Ó Bhéal, and artwork featured in t'ART online.

John McCullough lives in Hove. His third book of poems, *Reckless Paper Birds* (Penned in the Margins) won the 2020 Hawthornden Prize for Literature, as well as being shortlisted for the Costa Poetry Award. Previous collections have been Books of the Year for the *Guardian* and the *Independent,* and he also won the Polari First Book Prize. His poem "Flower of Sulphur" was shortlisted for the 2021 Forward Prize for Best Single Poem. His fourth collection, *Panic Response,* was published in March 2022 by Penned in the Margins.

JP Seabright is a queer disabled writer living in London. They have six solo pamphlets published and four collaborations, encompassing poetry, prose, and experimental work. They have been nominated for a Pushcart Prize, Forward Prize, and shortlisted (twice) for a Saboteur Award for Best Collaborative Work. They are co-editor of the *eff-able* anthology.

Karl Knights' poetry has appeared in the Forward Book of Poetry 2024. He won the 2021 New Poets Prize. His debut pamphlet, *Kin,* appeared in 2022. He lives in Suffolk.

Katie (Tom) Walters is a nonbinary poet making work about love and compost. They are deeply interested in the transformative and the weird, writing strange words about the historically fraught relationship between disabled bodies and nature.

Libro Levi Bridgeman wrote the sell-out theatre show *The Butch Monologues.* Short stories include "For Ezra", now a stop-motion film. They co-run hotpencil press with Serge Nicholson. They are featured in the doco "Private View".

Madailín Burnhope (she/her) is a widely published Disabled, transfemme writer from Warwickshire, UK. Her poem "You Wouldn't Last Five Minutes as a Woman" was Highly Commended in the 2024 Forward Prizes.

Marlena Chertock is a disabled, lesbian, Jewish poet with two books of poetry, *Crumb-sized: Poems* and *On that one-way trip to Mars.* She uses her skeletal dysplasia as a bridge to scientific poetry.

Max Wallis is a poet and journalist exploring queerness, survival, and mental health. Max is the founder of *The Aftershock Review,* a new poetry magazine devoted to exploring the aftershocks of experience.

POET BIOS

Mollie Russell is a bisexual autistic poet and journalist living in Wales. Her poems often explore gender and disability through the lenses of pop culture and monstrosity.

nat raum is the Editor in Chief of fifth wheel press. They're the author of *this book will not save you* and many others.

Petra Kuppers is a German disability culture activist and community performance artist. Her fourth poetry collection is the true crime/ecopoetry-themed *Diver Beneath the Street* (2024). She teaches at the University of Michigan.

Rae White is the queer-trans author of award-winning poetry collections *Milk Teeth* and *Exactly As I Am*. Their debut picture book *All the Colours of the Rainbow* is out now.

Raman Mundair FRSL is an Indian-born, director, writer, artist, activist, filmmaker, and playwright. They are a graduate of the National Film and Television School and were shortlisted as a writer and director for BFI Sharp Shorts. Raman was longlisted for the Rolex Mentor and Protégé Arts Initiative Award, and the Margaret Tait Award, and is a winner of the Robert Louis Stevenson Award and a recipient of both an ALL3Media Scholarship and a Leverhulme Fellowship.

Rebecca Kenny (she/her) is a pansexual poet and education consultant from Cheshire. She is dedicated to increasing equity in both education and the arts, and is the Founder of Written Off Publishing, a small press amplifying marginalised voices.

Rick Dove is a black, queer, and disabled writer from South London. Widely anthologised since 2016, Rick became UK Poetry Slam Champion in 2021, and has published two solo collections.

Rosamund Taylor's collection, *In Her Jaws* (Banshee Press, 2022), was shortlisted for the Seamus Heaney Poetry Prize for a First Collection and longlisted for the Polari First Book Prize

Sara Cline is a poet, comedian, University of Washington MFA alumna, and recipient of an Academy of American Poets Prize. Sara was born and bred in Plano, Texas.

Scarlett Ward is the Staffordshire Poet Laureate 2024–26. She was shortlisted for the Women Poets' Prize 2022 and works as Editor in Chief at Fawn Press Publishing.

Tallon Kennedy is a chronically ill queer poet, scholar, and teacher from Columbus, Ohio. Their poetry has been published in *Frontier Poetry, Rust + Moth,* and *The Mantle.*

Will Darling is an artist, writer, and transsexual menace. He is the author of *Gay Cabin* and lives in Seattle, Washington.